MW01120497

It's My Pleasure to Measure the Treasure!

Kelly Doudna

Consulting Editors, Diane Craig, M.A./Reading Specialist
and Susan Kosel, M.A. Education

Published by ABDO Publishing Company, 4940 Viking Drive, Edina, Minnesota 55435.

Printed in the United States.

Credits
Edited by: Pam Price
Curriculum Coordinator: Nancy Tuminelly
Cover and Interior Design and Production: Mighty Media
Photo Credits: AbleStock, Comstock, Kelly Doudna, Photodisc, ShutterStock, Wewerka Photography

Library of Congress Cataloging-in-Publication Data

Doudna, Kelly, 1963-
    It's my pleasure to measure the treasure! / Kelly Doudna.
      p. cm. -- (Science made simple)
    ISBN 10 1-59928-602-5 (hardcover)
    ISBN 10 1-59928-603-3 (paperback)

    ISBN 13 978-1-59928-602-0 (hardcover)
    ISBN 13 978-1-59928-603-7 (paperback)
    1. Weights and measures--Juvenile literature. I. Title. II. Series: Science made simple (ABDO
Publishing Company)

    QC90.6.D68 2007
    530.8--dc22

                                                                    2006015233

SandCastle Level: Transitional

SandCastle™ books are created by a professional team of educators, reading specialists, and content developers around five essential components–phonemic awareness, phonics, vocabulary, text comprehension, and fluency–to assist young readers as they develop reading skills and strategies and increase their general knowledge. All books are written, reviewed, and leveled for guided reading, early reading intervention, and Accelerated Reader® programs for use in shared, guided, and independent reading and writing activities to support a balanced approach to literacy instruction. The SandCastle™ series has four levels that correspond to early literacy development. The levels help teachers and parents select appropriate books for young readers.

Emerging Readers　　**Beginning Readers**　　**Transitional Readers**　　**Fluent Readers**
(no flags)　　　　　　　(1 flag)　　　　　　　　(2 flags)　　　　　　　　(3 flags)

These levels are meant only as a guide. All levels are subject to change.

When you **measure**, you use a tool to find information such as length, weight, time, or temperature. Tools such as rulers, scales, clocks, and thermometers are used to measure. You can also use everyday objects to measure.

Words used to talk about measuring:

amount	scale
clock	temperature
height	thermometer
length	time
measuring cup	volume
ruler	weight

I use a ruler to measure the length of my .

I can also use a ruler to measure the length of a .

I use a  to measure the weight of my .

A thermometer measures the temperature to which the ☀ has warmed the air outside.

7

I use a to measure the amount of vegetable oil to use for my .

A  measures

how much time it takes

to bake my .

It's My Pleasure to Measure the Treasure!

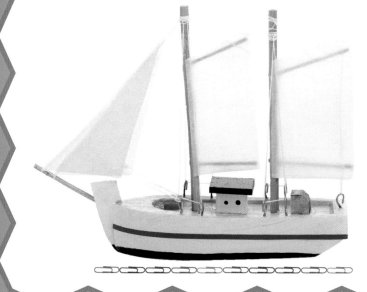

A guy named Ray spends his days measuring things in different ways. Ray thinks it's hip to use paper clips to measure his toy ship.

When I lay the clips end to end, it takes about ten.

12

Next Ray uses
sunflower seeds.
He wants to see
how many he needs
to measure the elf
that sits on his shelf.

The elf is quite small.
It is 12 sunflower
seeds tall.

14

Finally, Ray finds that three rocks weigh the same as seven blocks. He has lots of fun seeing how it can be done.

It's my pleasure to measure the treasure!

15

We Measure Every Day!

Marcus is making pancakes. He uses a measuring cup to measure the correct amount of flour to use.

A measuring cup measures volume. Volume is the amount of space something takes up.

17

Hannah has an alarm clock. It beeps when it is time for her to wake up.

A clock measures how much time has passed.

19

Max has a giant apple.
He uses a scale to
measure its weight.

Weight is a
measurement of
how heavy
something is.

The nurse measures Helen's height and weight at her checkup.

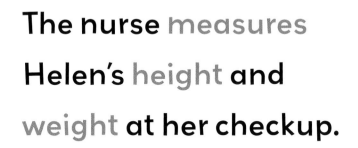

How would you measure different things around you?

Glossary

amount – how much there is of something.

length – the distance from one end of an object to the other.

ruler – a tool used to measure length.

scale – a tool used to measure weight.

temperature – a measure of how hot or cold something is.

thermometer – a tool used to measure temperature.